"I hold the Lion's Paw

Whenever I dance.

I know the ecstasy of the falcon's wings

When they make love against the sky…"

❀

HAFIZ—14TH CENTURY

(Trans. Ladinsky)

ISBN 978-0-9885080-0-2
Library of Congress Control Number: 2012952805
Printed in the United States of America
Published by FalconWings Inc.
P.O. Box 8923
Briarcliff Manor, NY 10510

Quotations: From letters written by Shri Brahmananda Sarasvati to js (1963–1970)

Book title and excerpt on page 3: From the poem "I Hold the Lion's Paw" from the Penguin publication *The Gift: Poems by Hafiz,* copyright © 1999 Daniel Ladinsky and used with his permission

Drawings: Blossom Folb (1998)
Cover and Book Design: Barbara Cooper
Photography of Drawings: Kelvin Jones

Dedicated to Shri Brahmananda Sarasvati
(Dr. Ramamurti S. Mishra)

you are attuned with me and
molded with me. So whatever
you feel that I also feel

I thought at first he was only a man, my Teacher.
But now I know he was, and is,
a Lion.
He wrote, "You are intuned with me and molded with me.
So, whatever you feel, that I also feel."
I did not understand these words when they were first written.
I understand them now.
Questions are asked. But it is not I that answers.

❀ ❀ ❀

js

"Desire for Self-analysis and

Self-analytical knowledge springs from

the thoughtful, rational, and logical mind

of man. Self-analytical philosophy

is not a luxurious type of thinking,

but is a natural flow of a thoughtful mind."

❀

SHRI BRAHMANANDA SARASVATI

QUESTION

How can I become more in tune with my soul so I can live out my mission in this life? How do I decipher what the soul is telling me and separate it from the thoughts? How do you let go of fear and attachment?

RESPONSE

Your mission in this life IS to be more in touch with your soul or Self. And all you need to accomplish this is to remove the thoughts that are blocking the soul itself. Just as clouds have to pass in order for the sun (that is always there) to be revealed.

The thoughts are the clouds that are covering the Self. Once the mind is empty of these thoughts, the Self, like the sun, which is self-luminous, instantly removes the darkness of ignorance. It is the mind that continues to produce those clouds of thoughts. And it would be foolish to use the same mind that is creating the thoughts in the first place to decipher them!

Remain very alert throughout your waking state and you will observe that your fear and feelings of attachment are the result of dwelling on the past or projecting into the future. If you clear your mind of past memories (even memories of five minutes ago) by means of the art of witnessing — which means being in the present moment — you will be able to instantly drop the thinking that has resulted in fear and attachment. We're either in the state of witnessing or thinking. It is the thinking that causes bondage, and it is witnessing that frees us.

"As long as dualism exists,

the enjoyment of life is imperfect.

The journey of perfection

and Self-realization begins

with love and ends with love."

❀

SHRI BRAHMANANDA SARASVATI

QUESTION

For as long as I can remember, I've desired a partner to share my life with. I cannot seem to let go of my need for a traditional relationship. Why do we seek partnership and companionship? For someone on a spiritual path, is this attachment and desire to find a lifelong companion one that needs to be overcome?

RESPONSE

According to the teachings, if, one day we are to be ultimately free, then *all* attachment and desires have to be dropped. But this state of desirelessness can only be attained when, by means of our own understanding, there has been a neutralization of these desires (and attachments), not because others have imposed their beliefs and desires upon us. It has to be a natural process.

Also, when you write that you've always wanted a "traditional" relationship with someone, this indicates that you still feel unfulfilled in this area. Which means you still need to have that type of relationship (and it's important that you do) before you can truly be convinced for yourself that nothing outside can ever bring the lasting happiness you seek.

Intellectual understanding will never satisfy us. That's why you shouldn't force yourself to live according to your mind or the minds of others. "Follow your bliss," Joseph Campbell said. It is not the mind that needs satisfaction, but the heart. Please don't try to repress these natural desires of yours. They are there for a reason. Let life present opportunities for you. Don't place yourself in a position where you lock yourself away from what your heart really desires. Let others be free to pursue their way of life, while you remain true to your own.

"The external tree of life is transformed

into the form of feelings, emotions and thoughts.

If there were no feelings and thoughts,

then what would we write? And if there were

no paper and ink, then on what

would they have been depicted and described?"

❀

SHRI BRAHMANANDA SARASVATI

QUESTION

Do you ever have any regret regarding past decisions?

———————

RESPONSE

One of the strongest messages of these teachings is that everything happens by itself, and those decisions we thought we had made all by ourselves were actually made by Nature — by destiny. And when it's time to move on, we simply move on. Having nothing to do with any determination on our part.

Ultimately, we realize that regrets have only to do with the past — and the past, being transitory, is not real. So, although the mind tends to nag us, our wisdom doesn't allow us to linger there. We're too focused on the "Now" to have regrets about what has happened before.

Whenever people came to Shri Brahmananda with sad problems related to their relative life, such as family, careers, relationships, etc., he would always say that these things were only temporary and would eventually pass away. He also explained that our life was merely a "drama" that has already been written — already in movement — according to our past karmas.

Shri Brahmananda would also remind us of Sri Ramana Maharshi's legendary statement to his own mother, "Whatever is destined not to happen will not happen. Whatever is destined to happen will happen, do what you may to stop it. This is certain. The best course, therefore, is for one to be silent."

And, this applies to having children — whether we're supposed to have them or not — careers, success, failure, relationships — everything! It's all preordained. And, although we imagine we're the ones deciding, making decisions and using our will to make things happen, all the enlightened ones tell us this is not the case.

According to them, everything depends on the Law of Cause and Effect, or the Law of Karma. They tell us we have no control over the actions or statements that occur. But we can be responsible for the motivations behind them and whether or not we choose to suffer as a result of these actions or statements.

So now it's up to you. You can choose to dwell on memories from the past and to project worries into the future. Or, you can decide to enjoy each and every moment of your life with all their ups and downs.

As stated by Sri Nisargadatta Maharaj, "Pain is inevitable. Suffering is optional."

"Behind every calamity, whether yesterday,

today or tomorrow, whether individual

or universal, whether national or international,

is a restlessness and lack of understanding —

a lack of discipline of our minds."

❀

SHRI BRAHMANANDA SARASVATI

QUESTION

My therapist has helped me accept that what I'm feeling is normal — a shock to my system, and that I am beating myself up for my reactions (sadness, despondency, indecision, etc.) to my wife's betrayal of my trust. How is it that we "seekers" have to endure such a shock to the system? Are we supposed to abandon our relative life to gain peace?

RESPONSE

Even in the Bhagavadgita, (Chapter 2), Lord Krishna tells
Arjuna, who is in a state of despair, that when desire and the
senses take over our wisdom, we are bewildered and lost.
And it is that which leads to our "destruction"— meaning the
destruction of our peace of mind.

It all comes down to desire. If you were able to accept (and
mind you, I'm not saying it's not hard) that this one period of
your life is over and not struggle to get it back, you wouldn't be
suffering so. Your wife's betrayal of your trust and asking for a
divorce must feel as if she and the life you knew have died, and
so you're going through a natural period of anger and grief.
This doesn't mean you have to give up on the pleasures you
receive from relative life. Not at all.

But it does mean you have to accept the reality of "Now" and
somehow move on. And yes, you and you alone have to do this.
There are many people who can urge you on and even stand by
you, but you're the one who has to walk on and not look back.

You can walk away from your wife and your former life with
her and know in your heart of hearts that if you're destined to be
with her again (even in this lifetime) it will happen without any
effort on your part.

"There is no choice between thinking and

not thinking — but choice is given only between

good thinking and bad thinking. No man

can live without any type of thinking.

Mind, like the sun, is awakened early morning

with the rays of thoughts, and like sunset at

the time of sleep, temporarily disappears into

the bottom of subconscious existence."

❀

SHRI BRAHMANANDA SARASVATI

QUESTION

I have been praying and asking to be shown the right path/direction I should take. I want to be true to myself and others around me, but I also want what I want out of life, and if I am completely honest I might lose my chance of having what I want. Can you give me some guidance regarding this problem?

RESPONSE

I remember that, in one of his talks, the great J. Krishnamurti spoke about decision-making. He indicated that if we found ourselves hesitant about making a decision, it meant that we were not capable of making a clear one at that time. Therefore, it would be best to wait. To do nothing until we had some degree of clarity and there was no longer any hesitation.

Shri Brahmananda said something similar. His advice was that before we even think about decisions that have to be made, we should first focus on being in a calm and peaceful state. He emphasized that our minds must be clear and quiet in order to see what is needed. Otherwise, if our thinking is desperate or panicky, we'll find ourselves making unwise decisions.

For example, you write that you're concerned about having a family before you "can't anymore." But, in the state of mind you're in right now, would you be able to create the best environment for your pregnancy or for those important, impressionable months of a newborn? That's why the sages always emphasize the importance of a calm and quiet mind.

My suggestion would be for you to reacquaint yourself with you — what you need to feel peaceful and unafraid. That's where meditation and the witnessing process come in. In the true state of meditation, there's a sense of peace and a quiet security.

As you continue to practice witnessing, slowly getting the knack of it, you'll find that you'll experience a greater sense of empowerment, gradually becoming less and less afraid of life and of making wrong decisions.

"If crying and weeping, tears and lamentations, sorrow and separation, were not presented by Nature, the suffering of this world might have been intolerable. And perhaps, due to the mighty weight of separation, the heart might have ceased to operate long before."

❀

SHRI BRAHMANANDA SARASVATI

QUESTION

I was really enjoying the message of your program tonight but then a strange thing happened on my way home. I felt on the verge of tears, and quite melancholy. Despite many people telling me I'm attractive, smart and funny, sometimes, like tonight, I just don't feel it. But, why tonight, after your talk? Why does a step forward feel like multiple steps back sometimes? Almost always out of balance?

RESPONSE

I think what I'm about to tell you is bound to surprise you.
It's something that Shri Brahmananda said to another young
woman who had the same reaction after hearing one of his talks.
He said, and I believe it without hesitation now, that the other
young woman had come so close to being directly in contact
with her own bliss, her own Truth, that the ego became alarmed
about its own existence continuing.

And so the ego went on the attack. Bringing up old haunting
fears, lack of confidence, tendencies of the mind to turn against
itself, renewal of doubts, questioning whether anything is truly
helping. The list goes on and on.

According to Shri Brahmananda, these powerful attacks of
self-doubting come only when you have come very close to
realizing the illusory nature of the so-called ego. They do not
signal a regression but rather a blossoming of your true life —
the life of total trust and bliss.

So, the best thing you can do is to stop thinking so much.
Just accept that you had a wonderful response to an extraordinary
Taoist reading, and also accept that this wonderful response was
followed by the old doubting mind (or ego) rebelling against what
it feels as its likely demise. You're better off letting both reactions
go — refusing to think about them at all — and simply going on
to the next experience that life is bound to present to you.

"We can reach by means of letters in

a short time and by means of telephone

we can talk sooner than a letter reaches.

But, by means of meditation, not only can we

talk but also we can become what we like

and can communicate in a single moment."

❀

SHRI BRAHMANANDA SARASVATI

In regard to the witnessing process, I am having a genuine difficulty in using such words as "I," "witness" and the phrase "I am the witness." I feel there is more clarity in using the word "one" or "this one" rather than the word normally referred to as "I" when in the state of witnessing. Same with saying something like "I am the witness." When one is truly witnessing, where is the "I"? Isn't there only awareness?

RESPONSE

Shri Brahmananda would say, "Yes! There is only awareness."

But then, if you stated that you have a genuine difficulty in using such words as I, mind, witness and the phrase I am the witness, he would smile and tell you not to use those words — but to use other words that would not give you difficulty.

And then I imagine he would say that any word — whether yours or his — is not going to give you the awareness or the tranquil mind that will allow the state of meditation to occur. The state in which all these distinctions, comparisons, likes and dislikes merge and dissolve into a feeling of Oneness.

In his essay *Peaceful Coexistence*, Shri Brahmananda wrote: "Everybody has his or her own universe. All want peace and peaceful coexistence on the level of the thinking mind, but that mind is the cause of all multiplicity, division and disunity. The witness is always beyond the body and mind. Be the witness.

Feel 'I have a body and mind, but I am not the body and mind. I am not the emotions.' *I AM THAT I AM.*"

Notice he's not saying we should *think* we have a body and mind but we are not the body and mind. He is saying we must *feel* this. He's also not saying to be the one *who is* the witness. He's saying *BE* the witness.

During the 30 years I was with Shri Brahmananda (while he was in his physical body), I heard him use many words to describe or explain the witnessing state and the state beyond the witnessing state. Sometimes he would say, "one" enters into the state of Pure Awareness. Or sometimes, the "I Am" merges into the state of Absolute Godhood.

After a while, we began to understand that he wasn't much interested in finding the words to best express that feeling — because that wasn't possible. Language is language and feeling is feeling.

Shri Brahmananda wanted us to have a taste of that state that was beyond the body and mind, beyond time and space. He wanted us to catch the fragrance of the unknown. And he told us emphatically that this could only occur when we were in the state of meditation beyond the thinking mind. His words: "Go beyond thinking into feeling — go beyond feeling into silence — go beyond silence into nothingness."

Eventually, we jump past the I and the one and even the witness and dive into the witnessing itself — wherein all our judgments and opinions disappear. And there's only *THATNESS.*

"By means of love and compassion, one reaches to identity of personality, which stands beyond the physical and mental plane. Without Divine Love, this state of identity with Supreme Consciousness cannot be obtained."

❀

SHRI BRAHMANANDA SARASVATI

QUESTION

I know that I should be grateful that I'm joyful, pretty, smart, and have wonderful people in my life. I know I'm really blessed, and for the most part, I do feel joyful in myself and not lacking or wanting. But, I don't know why I never have a boyfriend. Can you give me any insight into this?

RESPONSE

In 1998, when I was in New Delhi, an Indian friend introduced me to a very well-known and highly respected astrologer. That day, my friend had her chart done and afterwards told me the astrologer had expressed an interest in doing mine.

I asked if he could do my son's chart instead.

The astrologer agreed to do so and after reading it, told me that my son's chart was extraordinary, and that he was destined to be a powerful force — that his future was "golden."

I remember telling the astrologer that my son would be pleased to hear that, but something told me he would be unhappy if I didn't inquire as to whether he would meet his "soulmate" in this lifetime.

To my surprise, the astrologer said that this wasn't important for my son to know. When I pressed him, he said there would definitely be women present in my son's life but that they would not play a major role in his spiritual journey.

As I was thanking him and preparing to leave, he said with a smile, "When you see your son again, ask him this question: 'Would you rather be ruled by a woman or by the Higher Forces?' "

You're very attractive and charming and there's no doubt in my mind that there are other men still to come in this lifetime for you. Those with whom you still need closure — neutralizing. And that's why you were born with "plumage" (your beauty, charisma, magnetism) — to attract those who represent unfulfilled desires from past lifetimes.

But, in the end, when it counts most, I feel you too will realize that your strongest desire, your most passionate desire, is, and was, simply to find peace of mind. Through meditation, the gateway to this peace of mind, you will come to realize you don't need to attain happiness. Because you are *That* already. (So said Shri Brahmananda, and all the enlightened masters.)

"When we want to express

what we understand to each other,

we find that real expression is missing.

That missing principle can be expressed

only through silence of the heart —

when it is absolutely pure

and free from all relative thoughts."

❀

SHRI BRAHMANANDA SARASVATI

QUESTION

(Following a silent retreat weekend) By Sunday morning I was very, very empty — devoid of personality. It was a sort of invisible energy, just being. It didn't have the vast, expansive, light feeling I get when meditating — when I feel that I'm in my natural state. Which is the real, natural state? It was a bit sad and a feeling of distant energy on Sunday morning.

RESPONSE

According to the masters of Yoga-Vedanta philosophy, neither state would be considered your natural state. Our natural state is one in which we're not aware of being aware — the state of "Effortless Awareness" or "Pure Awareness."

When you're feeling expansive, light, empty, sad or devoid of personality, it indicates that there is a separate "I" judging how you feel. In other words, you're creating a sense of duality by labeling the feeling you're having.

Whereas, our natural state is a state of "Oneness," a non-dual state in which labels, comparisons, judgments, opinions and expectations all disappear.

Remaining as the *Witnessing-I* — just seeing what is — will allow you to be in your natural state of "Oneness," effortlessly and spontaneously.

You can even witness the mind's tendency to label, judge and compare, noticing that the witness remains aloof and undisturbed. Witnessing opens the gate to real meditation, where even the witness is dissolved into an ocean of bliss.

"The body, senses, mind and spirit have

some special meaning in addition to those

by which the world is using them.

This special meaning is to discover the unity

of the body, senses, mind and spirit.

As long as this unity is not realized, the body,

senses, mind and spirit run in various

different ways, and the mission of life remains

uncertain, unsettled and unaccomplished."

❀

SHRI BRAHMANANDA SARASVATI

QUESTION

My elder son is so used to always being first, getting more, and so needing that!

My husband and I were talking about it last night, and he pointed out that our son has been like that since he was a baby. Always greedy for things and attention; always fearful of not getting enough, of missing out on something. Then my husband said: "God knows what he was like last lifetime. I wonder what made him that way?" He's often very mean to his younger brother, who adores him, and is hurt by the way his brother treats him. Can you advise?

RESPONSE

I know Shri Brahmananda would have answered you in this way because this was his usual response when parents complained that their children were too self-concerned, too needy.

He would have said, "Not only does God know what he was like last lifetime, but both you and your husband also know. Because you were his parents last lifetime and perhaps other lifetimes, as well!"

He would have gone on to say that both of you, as his parents in this and past lifetimes, did not give him enough attention or enough love, and that he never felt — even as a baby — that he was No.1 (which is a baby's entitlement). And so, he has returned to you again because you owe him this. He wants more now because in the past (other lifetimes), he always received less.

When we're children, this is the one time that we should expect to have our needs come before those of our parents. And each of us needs to have at least two or three years of being No. 1. In your son's case, in this present incarnation, he lost out again. Because even if he had tasted that joy for a short period of time — before his baby needs could be truly satisfied — along came his younger brother. And so, although not having had his fill of being No.1 and still unsatisfied, he had to yield to the new baby. And then he was expected to be the big brother, while still a needy baby himself.

No wonder he's hungry for more, still needs more. He has never been given his rightful due.

It's certainly no fault of his that he's so needy. He was conditioned to be that way. It's not fair to expect him to "work through his insecurities." If he was born with insecurities, it's because others' behavior has caused him to be that way.

By the way, parents also do the best they can, but they aren't always able to place their children's needs before their own. And that's because their own parents had not been able to do this for them.

It may take a while, but I feel that if your son is given enough respect and a sense of being loved unconditionally (regardless of his behavior), he will finally be able to move past his former neediness. And his fear of "missing out on something."

"*Every man understands himself*
very wise but if he is really wise,
he should never suffer. When he begins
to suffer, then he experiences the bankruptcy
of wisdom. So, wise is he who
is established in his own Self.
He is beyond suffering and sorrow."

❀

SHRI BRAHMANANDA SARASVATI

QUESTION

My life is full. I am busy and seem to be of service. I am grateful and content in so many ways. However, I have become acutely aware as of late that I am being deeply affected by the people around me when I am not working. Any slight insult or oversight, real or imagined, physical or energetic, has been shaking me. I am witnessing this, noticing the pain in my belly, then moving forward with my day. Still I feel the ghosts of these blows. Can you offer me any advice regarding this?

RESPONSE

If you were an ordinary person with ordinary sensitivity, I could simply advise you to take more breaks during the day, find time for a short walk, go on mini-vacations, and be sure to reserve 15 minutes a day to meditate or listen to a relaxation CD that works for you.

But you're not an ordinary person with ordinary sensitivity. You are someone with exceptional skills, talents and a powerful mind, but also an extraordinary sensitivity. And in my view, this super-sensitivity, extreme vulnerability, is at the root of your reacting in such an extreme way to even the slightest indication of criticism or negative feelings toward you. That's why all that you're doing to relax and free yourself of unwanted thoughts is not proving enough to shake off these extreme reactions you're having.

So, what to do about this problem?

If you awakened tomorrow and your body had symptoms of a cold coming on, you would take ordinary precautions, such as cutting down on your exercise programs, avoiding getting chilled, eating lightly, etc. But, suppose you awoke with symptoms of pneumonia? Immediately, you would know that you need to have a chest X-ray, consult with a doctor and be prepared to offer your body a long, healing period of rest and rehabilitation. You would know that extreme measures would have to be taken.

(continued)

What would further complicate matters for you would be if your doctor were to tell you that, unfortunately, your medical history indicates you have a predisposition for contracting pneumonia and that there's no vaccine that can help.

Then, you would have to consider a serious change in your lifestyle — one that is, as much as possible, free of undue physical or emotional stress and strain.

In my view, overly sensitive people have to think of themselves in the same protective manner as if their bodies were prone to pneumonia. Meaning, it is not only preferable, but absolutely necessary that they avoid the strain of a stressful job, the company (or telephone calls) of anyone whose language or presence causes tension and anxiety — and even avoid reading books or watching television shows that are of a stressful nature.

In other words, treat your symptoms of being overly sensitive as if they were symptoms of pneumonia. Avoid, at any cost, all forms of stress. Even good forms of stress — like planning for a wedding, addressing large audiences, socializing too often with groups of friends, etc. — can be a cause for alarm when you're overly sensitive.

Sometimes, what is needed most is to be completely alone for at least an hour every day — away even from your loved ones.

Aloneness and silence — doing nothing but gazing at the sun setting at the end of the day — can be amazingly healing and empowering.

All of this really means a brand-new look at your current lifestyle. Just a few changes that serve to simplify and bring more moments of quiet into your everyday life can pave the way to your feeling much happier and much more in control.

Pneumonia cannot be cured by relaxation or self-help techniques. Nor can an overly sensitive nature.

"*Although we may have a thousand doubts and suspicions, a thousand evils, still we forgive this mind and can live easily and peacefully with it. If we can forgive all sins of our own mind, then it is very easy to forgive and forget the sins of others. The greatest enemy is the mind and the greatest hell is the mind. Nobody is the cause of troubles in this world. Mind is the cause.*"

❀

SHRI BRAHMANANDA SARASVATI

QUESTION

Everything around me has been and is continuing to fall apart.
I have lost all my savings as a result of all the negative events
that have been happening to me. Every day there seem to be more
and more problems and I feel as though I might have a nervous
breakdown. I go to bed depressed, hoping that the following day
will be better. All of my positive strategies for strength are failing
me. I'm really trying to hang in there but I'm getting close to the
end of my strength. What should I do?

RESPONSE

Something tells me that what you're regarding as a curse is really a blessing.

When Shri Brahmananda's students had periods in their lives when they were enjoying their families, their careers, and so forth and so on, some of them often stopped coming to his programs, and a number of them no longer felt a need to seek his guidance and counsel.

But when life turned against these students and everything turned negative and bitter, that's when they returned to Shri Brahmananda, seeking his grace, seeking comfort.

His advice during those hard and challenging periods was always the same. He told those who were suffering "to stay close to the teachings and to meditate — beyond the body, mind and senses."

Shri Brahmananda reminded us many, many times of the following: As long as we are not really challenged by life, we run the risk of remaining spiritually asleep. But once we are faced with despair, which is considered the dark night of the soul for the seeker, then we are forced to be awake.

To stay afloat in the turbulent waters of challenging times, we need to do our best to wait and to trust. Once the trust is there, you will find that you are automatically attracting positive and magnetic energy your way — the energy that will allow you to overcome all your difficulties.

The key word is trust.

"The common man is familiar only with that type of mind which is called conscious mind. The other existence of mind, such as subconscious, preconscious, unconscious and super-conscious, are unknown to him. But, by means of self-analysis, all existences of mind become visible to the conscious mind. And when this mind, as a whole, is recognized and realized, the light becomes wonderful and the essence of the seeker becomes eternal and immortal."

❀

SHRI BRAHMANANDA SARASVATI

QUESTION

Ramana Maharshi has stated, "In sleep man is devoid of all possessions, including his own body. Instead of being unhappy, he is quite happy." But you're unconscious when you are sleeping. Does this mean in order to be happy we must remain unconscious?

RESPONSE

The enlightened masters ask, "If we are really 'unconscious' while we are sleeping, then how do we know when we awaken in the morning that we slept well or badly or had a lovely dream?"

That we are aware of these different happenings tells us that although the body may be sleeping, Consciousness is still present. The enlightened are aware of the presence of Consciousness in deep sleep, whereas the ordinary person is not. Once you're established in the meditative state, you too can become aware of your body sleeping, while the *Witnessing-I* remains awake.

We all love to sleep soundly. And Sri Ramana Maharshi takes this as proof that our dreamless sleep state resembles our natural state — a state in which we are happiness itself.

"How to be alone to experience bliss and

the embrace of eternity is the universal problem.

Our whole search, whether by recognized way

or with un-recognized way, is the pursuit

of happiness, which is nothing but Self, Itself.

Hence, direct search becomes more

and more meaningful, and it avoids the

long journey of the Spirit."

❀

SHRI BRAHMANANDA SARASVATI

QUESTION

How do I become what I feel is already within me?

RESPONSE

According to Yoga-Vedanta teachings, all that is preventing you from becoming what is within is simply the notion that you need to become something other than what you are already.

This is called wrong identification with the body, mind and senses — the body/mind entity. This mistaken identification is caused by wrong thinking. Imagining that the emotionally scarred, conditioned personality is what you are.

Right identification is with that which is unchanging, without blemish.

In the beginning, this unchanging entity is experienced as the *Witnessing-I*. Later on, when you're more established in the witnessing state, even this identification is dissolved and all sense of duality or difference drops away.

Then there's no ego-mind or "judge" to prevent us from feeling a sense of "Oneness" with the entire universe. And with everyone who is part of our life.

"Constantly meditate on sound current

and transform the physical form of

body into the vibration of sound.

You will find the entire universe melting

into the ocean of consciousness.

The entire universe will be experienced

like the concentrated form of ideas

as ice is the concentrated form of water."

❀

SHRI BRAHMANANDA SARASVATI

QUESTION

I am able to hear the inner ringing sound (the inner sound current) when I meditate, but what am I supposed to do with that ringing sound?

RESPONSE

What if I said to you, "I was listening to Mozart last night and I remember that while I was listening I was able to forget everything and just be 'blissful' during that time? But, what am I supposed to do with that lovely memory of Mozart's music and the impact it had on me?"

I'm sure you would say that I shouldn't try to do anything with that memory, other than to enjoy it.

The inner sound current is eternally with us — as the space around us is constantly with us. And, this inner music is so compelling, that when we allow ourselves to be absorbed by it, we're immediately transported to a different dimension — beyond the body, mind and senses, beyond time and space.

On that plane, all our (imagined) earthly problems disappear and a mysterious transformation occurs. I say "mysterious" because that's what Shri Brahmananda called it. He stated that on that plane the body and mind are mysteriously healed and rejuvenated.

So, there's no need to "do" anything with the ringing sound. Each time you're aware of that sound, just keep focusing on it. No matter how many times your mind pulls you away, keep returning your focus there. After a while, you will feel its healing influence.

"It is true that everybody has to do

his own practice of meditation,

and enlightenment of one will not enlighten

the other. But it is equally true that,

in reality, there is no otherness.

There is nobody to exist independently.

It is the one Being who is reflecting

through all becomings; still, this Being

does not go into any change."

❀

SHRI BRAHMANANDA SARASVATI

QUESTION

As these teachings reflect truths about the world and ourselves, why are only the minority called to them? Isn't this where everyone is going, and why are we in such a minority?

RESPONSE

The teachings point out that it is desires — unfulfilled desires — that are the cause of our continuing to be drawn back to the world, lifetime after lifetime. Fortunately, we're also drawn back to the truths that will ultimately set us free.

Having been involved with these teachings and the difficulties that seekers face along their journey, I've observed that although people tend to begin their spiritual journey with great enthusiasm (mainly because it gives them some hope that they can change their lives for the better), very few of them have the perseverance and the "readiness" to maintain that enthusiasm.

As the great teachers often say, "There are many givers on this journey but few takers."

Shri Brahmananda also said, "It works when you are ready."

Then too, many people stay with the teachings until they feel a little better or have a greater sense of control. They regard meditation as more of a relaxation and a clearing — rather than a gateway to Self-realization and freedom. Eventually, each of us will be drawn back to our original, desireless state, which is the state of perfection.

But, until we've had even a taste of it, we're told we have to rely on the testimony of the great masters to keep us relentlessly on our journey.

"Suspicions and doubts shall be

the nature of the mind. Mind cannot live

without them. But it is the Spirit

which is victorious over this mind

and not the mind itself. Spirit becomes

victorious just once and once

it becomes victorious, it remains

permanently victorious."

❀

SHRI BRAHMANANDA SARASVATI

QUESTION

Learning who I am in relation to people is quite difficult. I feel that people are ashamed of me. I don't know where "home" is. I'm alone and can't seem to fight — nor flee — nor keep peace. I don't know how to love. Or so it feels. I don't know and am criticized every step of the way. It's excruciating. What do I do?

RESPONSE

I'm sorry you've been going through so much pain. Psychological pain is far more damaging than physical. But, according to Shri Brahmananda and all the great masters, these "shocks" are often what are necessary to wake us up from the dream that the thinking mind presents as reality.

In reality, there is no conflict, no loneliness, no guilt, no shame, no frustration — because in the state of "No-mind," where there are no memories of the past nor projections into the future, we are in our natural state of peace and non-conflict, our natural state of unconditional love and compassion.

We cannot "work on" being in that state because like the sun, it is always present. Never missing. But, we can remain ever-vigilant, awake as much as possible, in order to catch the thinking mind when it is interfering with our natural feeling of bliss and well-being.

All that is needed to be in that natural state of effortless awareness, our natural state of meditation, so we can live without conflict of any kind, is a quiet mind.

Therefore, ridding ourselves of unnecessary thinking is our most important task of every minute of our waking state. Sri Nisargadatta Maharaj (from the book, *I AM THAT*,) has stated that when we find ourselves struggling with negative forces and circumstances during our lives, it's best to just let things happen by themselves and not continuously try to find solutions to end the struggle. There are times, he said, we simply have to endure and patiently wait for the difficult period to pass.

"A majestic and glorious life

is nothing but a disguised form of death

if it leads us to the state of ignorance.

And even the tragic form of life is nothing

but a disguised form of heaven and bliss

if it leads us to enlightenment and knowledge.

But when tragedy and majesty both

lead to enlightenment and liberation —

that is the best."

❀

SHRI BRAHMANANDA SARASVATI

BFell

QUESTION

How committed should I be to a particular path? Or can I pick and choose among them? Can I have more than one guru? Or am I just being indecisive?

RESPONSE

You should go where your heart leads you at a particular time. When I first met Shri Brahmananda, his approach to Yoga-Vedanta was scientific and intellectual. That was in the 1960s.

And then, in the early 1970s, he introduced his students to the Agni Hotra fire ceremony and Indian mythology, and encouraged observance of special commemorations of Indian holy days. Following his stroke in 1983, Shri Brahmananda placed greater emphasis on the study of Sanskrit, the scriptures and Vedic chanting.

However, his main focus was always on the deepening of meditation, the practice of self-inquiry, the art of witnessing and an in-depth study of Yoga-Vedanta teachings. Shri Brahmananda also placed a strong emphasis on the need for practical application in our everyday life.

Throughout all these different approaches, Shri Brahmananda was also introducing us to the teachings of other masters, such as Lord Buddha, Sri Ramana Maharshi, Sri Nisargadatta Maharaj, Krishnamurti, Rajneesh (Osho), great Taoist and Zen masters, and many, many others.

And now, almost 50 years later, I still return from time to time to all these masters, according to my specific needs at a particular time. Shri Brahmananda taught us that any enlightened master whose teaching serves to free us from suffering and ignorance is serving as our "Guru" for that specific time in our lives.

According to Shri Brahmananda, all of these great masters are offering the same message by means of different approaches. That message being: To have as our ultimate goal the discovery that we are already free, already enlightened.

All we need is to stop identifying with the body/mind entity and recognize once and for all, *I AM THAT I AM!*

"As the flow of the river disappears

in the sea, losing its name and form,

so a wise man, freed from name and form,

goes to the divine person who is beyond all.

Ultimate reality is itself nothing but

true and pure love, which is nothing

but Pure Spirit."

❀

SHRI BRAHMANANDA SARASVATI

QUESTION

I think Ramana Maharshi's idea of whatever happens is meant to happen can be misrepresented as no effort is needed to evolve. What do you think?

RESPONSE

Sri Ramana Maharshi also said, "All the activities that the body is to go through are determined when it first comes into existence. It does not rest with you to accept or reject them. The only freedom (free will) you have is to turn your mind inward and renounce activities there."

People will interpret the various statements of masters according to their level of understanding. That's why Shri Brahmananda warned against interpretation, saying that all interpretations originate from the mind, and for truth to be realized, the mind must be transcended. Realizing this, the enlightened ones respond to each questioner on the level of his or her understanding. My own direct experience is in accordance with Shri Brahmananda's statement, "Real life does not begin until your sense of *I AM* is in the witnessing state."

The witnessing state opens the door to our natural state of meditation.

"We wish to tell something extremely important and unique, but what it is we don't know. The mind can cognize that, but it cannot write (that). The tongue can express and the hand can write — but they have never experienced that Bliss."

❈

SHRI BRAHMANANDA SARASVATI

QUESTION

The Masters seem very interested/concerned with nuclear war and power. I share that concern. What exactly does it mean to them spiritually? Total destruction?

RESPONSE

The great masters tell us that the wars that are going on outside are only reflections of the wars that are going on within us. And that if we are really concerned with peace in the world, we must first find peace in our own hearts, inwardly. When our minds are quiet and free of divisive thinking, we can experience this unifying thread of consciousness — the sense of Oneness with all.

If the planet is destined to be destroyed, it will be. But that destruction should be due to natural forces — not the forces of hatred and divisiveness.

Throughout his life, this was one of Shri Brahmananda's essential teachings.

A LETTER FROM RAMAMURTI S. MISHRA
(Shri Brahmananda Sarasvati)

November 30, 1970

Greetings.

My relation with you is the relation of oneness and not the relation of even Guru and student. No doubt, some people feel that by having a Guru, and having contact with a master, they will be insured for liberation in this very incarnation. The importance of Guru and disciple lies not so much in the physical contact, but lies in understanding the nature of the Self and Self-realization. By understanding the nature of Consciousness, it is automatically understood that the Spirit is One without a second, although in the relative plane, one is the individual self, the other is the Guru, and the third is God.

What can Guru do, if he is enlightened? He can neutralize the disciple's karma and can give some important advice, which if followed, will enable the student to handle his inner nature and to recognize his consciousness in pure form, as God Consciousness. Also, the Guru can help in analyzing the experience, which remains otherwise unexplained and uninterpreted, even by the Shastras (scriptures).

The journey of the inner space is not like the journey of the motor car on the autobahn of Germany, or the refined road of the United States; but it is like the journey by jet plane, flying through the night of ignorance, clouded with doubts and skepticism and uncertainty, from known reality to unknown reality. This type of journey needs much more interpretation and understanding, and a competent and enlightened Guru can definitely illumine the mind of the student in these matters. Not only Guru, but even God cannot liberate disciples, without their cooperation. If it were so, then there could have been no lawlessness in the world, and the entire world could have been enlightened long ago.

Some students continue changing gurus from time to time, or searching a guru with long beard and moustache and with funny dress. Some of them are keeping pictures like that without knowing the real person who the pictures represent. Some are very restless in search of a master higher than the one they have — instead of living by the simple rules already given by their guru.

No doubt, it is extremely helpful and uplifting to come into contact with an illumined Guru, especially with an enlightened one. In any case, we must not forget that a guru does not have a distinct light, which does not exist in the student. God is sleeping in all equally, and it is not on the part of God and Guru, but on the part of student — how much work he can do to awaken his sleeping spirit, which is nothing but God. It is not really God who is sleeping in us; on the contrary it is our mind which is sleeping to God, who is eternally shining in us. Hence, it is not a matter of making the light shine, but it is a matter of experiencing the shining light.

Enlightened men taught us, teach us, and will teach us the truth, if we approach them in a spirit of innocent and sincere enquiry. Until one realizes the light within oneself, one must continue to work hard, according to the advice of those who have had the true experience of God. Neither should one accept blindly what is offered, nor should one offer a blind path of spirituality, about which, one is never certain on the name of certainty. Today, there are many teachers who require of their students blind obedience. "Such teachers think that death of the intellect is the condition of the spiritual life" (Dr. Radhakrishnan).

One must use reason and logic to evaluate the facts of life and experience. "Doors and windows of our house should be open to receive good persons and fresh air, but we must stand firmly so that we should not be blown away through those open windows and we should not fall into the false dogmas of our friends" (M.K. Gandhi).

One need not be dumb to be successful on the spiritual path. The truth is beyond intellect and intelligence, but it is not below them. Many simple-minded people are drawn to such teachers who are offering precarious or ready-made enlightenment. They are not so much drawn to them by their spiritual power, but by the publicity and propaganda of their agents.

It is possible to rest in God-Consciousness within the framework of current customs and appearances, with common life and uncommon insight into the nature of life and ultimate truth…Sometimes silence stops us to tell what we wish to tell…Everything is in the hands of Nature, and it will happen what is destined to be happened by Supreme Nature.

— *Ramamurti S. Mishra*

SHRI BRAHMANANDA SARASVATI

Shri Brahmananda Sarasvati, also known as Ramamurti S. Mishra, M.D., was a highly respected spiritual teacher for countless students and devotees from all walks of life. A prolific author on the science and philosophy of Yoga-Vedanta, he integrated the universal message of these teachings with his deep knowledge of both Eastern and Western medicine and psychology. His areas of specialty ranged from Ayurveda to modern psychiatry and neurosurgery.

Shri Brahmananda Sarasvati is the Founder and Spiritual Director of the Yoga Society of New York, Inc. (1958) and its country center Ananda Ashram (1964). He also established the Yoga Society of San Francisco, Inc. (1972), known as Brahmananda Ashram, and inspired several other centers of meditation in the United States and abroad.

He was a master of the Sanskrit language, and his lifework is considered a comprehensive and authentic modern synthesis of the ancient teachings. His written works include *Fundamentals of Yoga, The Textbook of Yoga Psychology* (a commentary on Patanjali's *Yoga Sutras*), *Self Analysis and Self Knowledge* (on Shankaracharya's *Atma Bodha*), translations of Upanishads and other ancient Sanskrit texts, as well as numerous essays and stories. In addition, much of his teaching exists in recorded form.

His life was dedicated to the integration of Eastern and Western sciences, culture and philosophy, and he presented the timeless message of meditation and Self-realization in a truly contemporary form. Shri Brahmananda Sarasvati left his physical body in 1993, yet his spiritual presence and teachings continue to be a source of inspiration and guidance for all.

With deep appreciation

and gratitude to Blossom Folb

for contributing her beautiful

drawings, which serve so well

as a bridge between the

unmanifest and the manifest.

* * *

BLOSSOM FOLB

The work of award-winning artist Blossom Folb has been exhibited in museums and galleries throughout the world, and she has been recognized with numerous awards, including the Heydenryk Prize, the Lena Newcastle Prize and the Aileen O. Webb Prize.

Ms. Folb's work has been represented in many influential group and one-person shows in the United Kingdom; France; and Malaga, Spain. The Roerich Museum, the Forum Gallery, and the Marble Arch Gallery in New York City, as well as the Landau Gallery in Los Angeles, have displayed her work.

Her work was also shown in the American Pavilion at the 1965 World's Fair in New York. She is represented in many corporate and private collections throughout the United States, including the American Museum of Printmaking in Albany, New York.

Ms. Folb is listed in Who's Who of American Women (1974-75 Edition), Two Thousand Women of Achievement, and the Dictionary of International Biography (1973-74 Edition). She is a life member of the National Association of Women Artists.

A native of New York City, Ms. Folb currently resides in Santa Monica, California.

ACKNOWLEDGMENTS

Marvin Suval

Karen Cook

Robert Jaeger

Tracie Martyn

Marius Morariu

Monica Pa Moye

• • •